RENEWED CHARM OF GUANGZHOU

新彩广州

广州市文化广电旅游局　南方日报社 | 编

Edited by

Guangzhou Culture, Radio, Television and Tourism Bureau

Nanfang Daily

南方日报出版社

NANFANG DAILY PRESS

中国 · 广州

图书在版编目（CIP）数据

新彩广州：汉英对照 / 广州市文化广电旅游局，南方日报社编. -- 广州：南方日报出版社，2025.1

ISBN 978-7-5491-2524-1

Ⅰ. ①新… Ⅱ. ①广… ②南… Ⅲ. ①地方文化—广州—汉、英 Ⅳ. ①G127.65

中国版本图书馆CIP数据核字（2022）第058395号

XINCAI GUANGZHOU

新彩广州

编　　者：广州市文化广电旅游局　南方日报社
出版发行：南方日报出版社
地　　址：广州市广州大道中289号
出 版 人：周山丹
责任编辑：张　高
封面设计：二间设计
内文设计：肖晓文
责任校对：阮昌汉
责任技编：王　兰
经　　销：全国新华书店
印　　刷：广东信源文化科技有限公司
开　　本：889mm × 1194mm　1/16
印　　张：15.25
字　　数：120千字
版　　次：2025年1月第1版
印　　次：2025年1月第1次印刷
定　　价：180.00元

投稿热线：（020）87360640　　读者热线：（020）87363865
发现印装质量问题，影响阅读，请与承印厂联系调换。

策划：刘瑜梅　侯小军

统筹：柯显东　陈韩晖

撰稿：周人果

翻译：杜可君　钟　慧

图片：（如有遗漏，请与出版单位联系）

陈碧信　彭延菁　邝健华　李锦显

马　华　孔剑锋　张　迪　吴伟洪

陈庆忠　石建华

杨毅衡 hunk

程贺彬（@Hobin-MK813）

广东省摄影家协会

视觉中国

FOTOE 图片库

Planners: Liu Yumei, Hou Xiaojun,

Co-ordinators: Ke Xiandong, Chen Hanhui

Written by: Zhou Renguo

Translators: Du Kejun, Zhong Hui

Photos by: (contact publisher if missing)

Chan Pik Shun, Pang Yin Ching, Kwong Kin Wah, Lee Kam Hin

Ma Hua, Kong Jianfeng, Zhang Di, Wu Weihong

Chen Qingzhong, Shi Jianhua

Yang Yiheng hunk

Cheng Hebin (@Hobin-MK813)

Guangdong Photographers Association

Visual China Group

FOTOE picture

PREFACE

GUANGZHOU REVITALIZED

- the Millennial Commercial Capital is Building a Better Life

序

新彩广州

——千年商都构筑美好生活

广州，作为中国的南大门，是中国走向世界的重要窗口。回望历史，这里曾万商云集、交流互鉴，开放包容、低调务实是这座千年商都的底色。她以敢为人先、务实创新的精神，塑造出日新月异的一方天地。

数千年来，广州吸引了全世界的商人造访，他们在这里觅到商机、创造财富。而今广州亦吸引着越来越多懂生活的人前来，他们在这里观光、休闲、度假、旅居，在“一盅两件”里品味惬意生活，在东山西关中触摸城市文脉，在一步一景中发现焕新的一天。

Guangzhou, as the gateway to South China, is a window for the country to the world. Looking back on its history, the city has gathered thousands of business people to conduct trade and learn from each other. Openness, inclusiveness and pragmatism are the signature of this millennial commercial capital. With its pioneering spirit, diligence and innovation, Guangzhou is changing with each passing day.

For thousands of years, Guangzhou has attracted merchants from all over the world, who have sought business opportunities and created wealth here. Today, it also attracts more and more people to enjoy their lives here: They come here to see, to relax, to travel or reside, to savor the pleasant life in "one cup and two pieces", to touch the city's cultural lineage in Dongshan and Xiguan, and to discover delightful surprises in every step.

今日广州之新，体现在城市面貌焕新颜。党的十八大以来，广州通过系统推进城市更新，全面提高土地利用效率，形成以调整重构为主、结构性拓展为辅的空间发展模式，为推动城市内涵集约式高质量发展，构建以国内大循环为主体、国内国际双循环相互促进的新发展格局，解决城市突出问题和短板、提升城市品质提供了有效路径。

今日广州之新，体现在文化生活焕新意。近年来，广州以文脉滋养城脉，以绣花功夫实现大城善治。截至2024年9月，广州拥有文化创意产业园和基地702个，国家级文化产业园区（基地）25个，文化上市公司49家，持续高标准打造红色文化传承弘扬示范区、岭南文化中心区和广州文化体制改革创新试验区，擦亮文化品牌。

今日广州之新，体现在生态空间焕新声。近年来，广州空气质量持续全面达标，“广州蓝”成为城市新名片。在云山珠水的庇佑下，当广州从清晨的第一缕阳光中苏醒，你只需闭眼聆听，便能听到来自城市与自然之间的灵动之声。

Guangzhou is taking on a new look. Since the 18th CPC National Congress, through promoting urban regeneration and enhancing the effectiveness of land use, the city has formed a spatial development model based on adjustment and reconstruction and supplemented by structural expansion, paving an effective path to push forward intensive and high-quality development, build a new development pattern with the domestic cycle as the mainstay and the domestic and international cycles promoting each other, solve the outstanding problems and shortcomings and improve the quality of the city.

The cultural life of Guangzhou is revitalizing. In recent years, the city has made efforts to boost its cultural sector and exercise good governance by paying attention to details. As of September 2024, it is home to 702 cultural and creative industry parks and bases, 25 national cultural industry parks (bases) and 49 listed cultural companies. Steps have been taken to build a demonstration zone for the inheritance and promotion of red culture, a Lingnan cultural center and a pilot area for the institutional reform and innovation of Guangzhou's cultural sector to polish its cultural brand.

Guangzhou's ecology is enhanced. In recent years, its air quality has met all standards, and "Guangzhou Blue" has become the city's new signature. When the first ray of the morning wakes up Guangzhou, you can hear the sounds of this livable city.

序
PREFACE

今日广州之新，体现在三餐四季焕新味。除广州人对“食”不变的信念之外，饮食业日益丰富的业态，为“美食天堂”提供了更充足的养料。近年来，从博古斯世界烹饪大赛落户广州，到米其林榜单入穗，从本土粤菜“走出去”到国际佳肴“引进来”，广州饮食文化不断展现其兼容并包、海纳百川的特质。

今日广州之新，体现在文旅消费焕新生。广州积极刺激文旅消费潜力，促进“夜经济”发展，从消费体验多元化向文旅商融合发展进化，从新消费场景多元化向新生活空间美化升级，为市民和游客创造主客共享的美好生活。

面向未来，广州将围绕建设“世界文化名城”和“世界级旅游目的地”总体定位，以挖掘、保护、传承、弘扬、活化优秀岭南传统文化为基础，突出岭南文化的特点特色，着力推动创新性发展、创造性转化。我们有理由相信，未来的广州不仅是拥有美丽风景、历史底蕴的千年古城，更是构筑美好生活的未来之城。

Guangzhou is embracing new development of its time-honored food culture. In addition to Guangzhou people's unswerving pursuit of food, the growing diversity of the food and beverage industry has provided this "Gourmet Paradise" with greater potential. In recent years, from the Bocuse d'Or to the Michelin list, from the going out of local Cantonese cuisine to the introduction of international food and beverage, Guangzhou's food culture has continued to show its inclusiveness and vitality.

Guangzhou's cultural and tourism consumption is revived. The city has been actively stimulating the potential of cultural and tourism consumption and advancing the "night economy". It evolves from providing diversified consumption experience to integrating culture, tourism and commerce, and upgrades from diversifying new consumption scenarios to constructing more beautiful new living spaces, hence creating a better life for both citizens and visitors.

Looking forward, oriented to its positionings as a "world famous cultural city" and a "world-class tourist destination", Guangzhou will investigate, protect, inherit, promote and revitalize the excellent Lingnan traditional culture, highlight its characteristics and drive innovative development and creative transformation. We have every reason to believe that Guangzhou is not only a thousand-year-old city with beautiful scenery and heritage, but also a city of tomorrow where a better life will be built.

编者　The Editors

2024年12月　December 2024

目　录
CONTENTS

新物
New Items

新意
New Ideas

IFC
ASCOTT
SPD BANK

新颜

New Look

新彩广州

RENEWED
CHARM
OF
GUANGZHOU

REVEALING A NEW LOOK OF THE MILLENNIAL COMMERCIAL CAPITAL THROUGH METICULOUS WORK

Guangzhou, the Flower City, blossoms from within and outside.

Thanks to its favorable climate, Guangzhou is a city of flowers in every season, and the winter here is still warm.

Always standing at the forefront of reform and opening up, the people of Guangzhou are shaping the old city with new vitality through pragmatic effort with great aspirations.

As the COVID-19 pandemic gives a test to a city's strength, Guangzhou has demonstrated the faith of its people, its force for good and its courage to take action in the trials and tribulations of the fight against the pandemic.

Time is a mirror that reflects the footprints of a city.

Guangzhou has shown its cultural confidence, its wisdom of governance and its ability to take action in the course of long history.

Taking a bird's eye view of this city, the steel forest cannot conceal the vibrant greenery, and the human touches are visible on Baiyun Mountain and Pearl River.

A closer look will reveal the classic charm of the old neighborhoods and the modern vitality of the new ones.

In recent years, Guangzhou has diligently studied and implemented the spirit of the 20th CPC National Congress and General Secretary Xi Jinping's important remarks and instructions during his visit to Guangdong, gathered the city's efforts to create new vitality of the old city, and achieved innovations in four areas, reinterpreting the thousand-year-old city's modern charm and foresight with embroidery-like detailed work.

“绣花”功夫见真招
千年商都展新颜

花城广州，内外兼修。

得气候之宜，广州花开四季冬日如春；

得风气之先，广州人民在务实生活与理想抱负间塑造着老城市新活力。

如果说疫情是城市实力的一次考验，

那么，广州在抗疫的磨砺中显现出一份人民的信仰、向善的力量、行动的魄力；

如果说时间是透视一座城市血脉的一面镜子，

那么，广州在历史长河中展现出一种文化的自信、治理的智慧、善为的能力。

俯瞰广州，“钢筋森林”中透着生机绿意，云山珠水间藏着人间烟火。

细细观览，老街区彰显经典魅力，新城区绽放时代活力。

一枝一叶总关情。近年来，广州牢记嘱托、感恩奋进，认真学习贯彻党的二十大精神和习近平总书记视察广东重要讲话、重要指示精神，举全市之力推进老城市新活力、“四个出新出彩”，以“绣花功夫”重新诠释一座千年古城的现代魅力和高远格局。

一眼千年

A Thousand Years at a Glance

新颜
New Look

北京路，广州古城中轴、千年商都核心。这里是海上丝绸之路的起点，延续着千年商都的文脉和无数老广的乡愁。

经过多年的提升改造，如今的北京路既传统又新潮。国内最大的户外裸眼3D屏幕吸引国内外游客驻足，五羊石像、南越王宫等广州知名地标徐徐展开，舞狮、广绣、打铜等广式非遗随着屏幕中古城墙开裂次第显现。

一条路或是一座城的缩影。传统与时尚交互，广府与国际交流，文化与商业交融。在这里，我们望见了一座街区的新颜，亦见证一座城市的包容与厚重。

Beijing Road is the central axis of the ancient Guangzhou city and the core of the millennial commercial capital. It serves as the starting point of the Maritime Silk Road, carrying the cultural lineage of this millennial city and the nostalgia of numerous Guangzhou residents.

After years of regeneration, Beijing Road is now both traditional and chic. Attracting visitors from home and abroad, the largest outdoor naked-eye 3D screen in China unfolds famous Guangzhou landmarks like the Five Goats Stone Statue and the Southern Yue Palace. Lion dance, Cantonese embroidery, brass making and other intangible cultural heritages of Guangzhou appear one after another as the ancient city wall cracks open in the screen.

A road can be a microcosm of a city. Here, the tradition and fashion intertwine, Guangzhou and the world meet, and culture and commerce mingle. Here, we see the new look of a neighborhood and witness the inclusiveness and richness of a city.

广州·越秀 / 南越王博物院

Guangzhou · Yuexiu / Nanyue King Museum

由原西汉南越王博物馆、原南越王宫博物馆合并组建的南越王博物院，在遗址保护的基础上，为公众提供一份多元、特色、优质的文化大餐，进一步擦亮“南越王”品牌。

Merging the former Western Han Nanyue King Museum and the Nanyue King Palace, the Nanyue King Museum provides the public with a diversified, distinctive and high-quality cultural feast along with preservation of the site, further polishing the Nanyue King brand.

◀

广州·越秀 / 五羊石像

Guangzhou · Yuexiu / Five Goats Stone Statue

位于越秀公园的五羊石像，主羊头部高高昂起，口中衔穗，回眸微笑，其余四羊环绕于主羊周围，或戏耍，或吃草。这一根据五羊传说创作的雕塑作品，自落成之日起便成为广州的城市标志。

The Five Goats Stone Statue in Yuexiu Park features the one in the middle holding its head high with ears of rice in its mouth and looking back smiling, while the other four surround it, either playing or eating grass. Created based on the legend of the five goats, this statue has always been the symbol of Guangzhou.

广州·荔湾 / 陈家祠

Guangzhou·Liwan / Chen Clan Ancestral Hall

陈家祠，集岭南地区多种建筑装饰工艺于一体，包括木雕、砖雕、石雕、陶塑、灰塑、铜铁铸和彩绘，被誉为“岭南建筑艺术的明珠”，是我国现存规模最大、保存最完好、装饰最精美的祠堂式建筑。其落成于清光绪十九年（1893年），是清代广东各地陈姓宗族在广州合资建造的合族祠。

Incorporating a variety of architectural decorative techniques in Lingnan area including wood carving, brick carving, stone carving, pottery sculpture, ash sculpture, copper and iron casting and color painting, the Chen Clan Ancestral Hall is the largest, best-preserved and most beautifully decorated ancestral hall in China, and is known as the "pearl of Lingnan architecture". Completed in the 19th year of Guangxu reign in the Qing Dynasty (1893), it was funded by the Chen clan from all over Guangdong during the Qing Dynasty.

新颜
New Look

广州·越秀 / 镇海楼

Guangzhou · Yuexiu / Zhenhai Tower

建于1380年的镇海楼五层相连、似塔似楼，是广州建城史的重要见证。镇海楼一身兼具文化史、军事史和博物馆史上的重要意义，在全国的名楼中独一无二。镇海楼正门旁的木棉高高耸立，疏叶浓花，像一把把艳丽的火炬。

As an important witness to the history of Guangzhou, the five-storied Zhenhai Tower, built in 1380, is unique among the country's famous buildings with its roles in the histories of culture, military and museum. Standing tall, the kapok trees by the main entrance of the tower are like blazing torches with their sparse leaves and blossoming flowers.

广州·越秀 / 中山纪念堂

Guangzhou · Yuexiu / Sun Yat-sen Memorial Hall

广州中山纪念堂是缅怀孙中山先生的重要遗迹，亦是广州市区拥有现代设备的政治、文化活动综合场所。这座中西合璧、兼具传统风格与现代功能的纪念堂，是广州最具代表性的城市地标之一。

Sun Yat-sen Memorial Hall is an important site in memory of Dr. Sun Yat-sen and a venue for political and cultural activities with modern facilities. Combining Chinese and Western elements, traditional styles and modern functions, this memorial hall is one of the most representative city landmarks of Guangzhou.

广州·越秀 / 北京路

Guangzhou · Yuexiu / Beijing Road

北京路，是广州建城2200多年来从未偏移、从未断代的城市中轴线，被冠以“千年城脉、广府商都”的美誉，见证着商业文明的更替与进步。

Beijing Road has remained Guangzhou's central axis for 2,200 years uninterruptedly since the city was founded. Known as the "Vein of the City for Thousands of Years and Commercial Center of Guangfu", Beijing Road has witnessed the evolution of the commercial civilization.

2021年7月，北京路正式被商务部评为“全国示范步行街”。随着一、二期改造工程的推进，它正在成为广州“老城市新活力”“国际消费中心城市”的重要展示窗口和具有世界影响力的岭南特色商圈。

In July 2021, Beijing Road was officially awarded the National Demonstrative Pedestrian Street by the Ministry of Commerce. With its first and second-phase renovation, Beijing Road is becoming a showcase of Guangzhou's "old city with new vitality" and "international consumption city" campaigns, as well as a business district with Lingnan characteristics and international influence.

广州·海珠 / 黄埔古港

Guangzhou · Haizhu / Huangpu Ancient Port

黄埔古港是十七、十八世纪中国海上贸易黄金时期的一个窗口。其作为中西方经济、文化交流的枢纽之一，见证了古代海上丝绸之路的繁荣。

Huangpu Ancient Port is a window to the golden age of Chinese maritime trade in the 17th and 18th centuries. As one of the hubs of economic and cultural exchanges between China and the West, it witnessed the prosperity of the ancient Maritime Silk Road.

广州·黄埔 / 南海神庙

Guangzhou · Huangpu / The Immortal Temple of South Sea

南海神庙是古代中国四大海神庙之一，是自隋始建至今国内留存最大的一座官祀海神庙，也是岭南建筑发展的历史见证。

The Immortal Temple of South Sea, one of the four major temples of the sea god in ancient China, has been the largest official temple of the sea god remaining in China since its construction in the Sui Dynasty, and a witness to the development of Lingnan architecture.

广州·黄埔 / 广州海事博物馆

Guangzhou · Huangpu / Guangzhou Maritime Museum

城央之魅

The Charm of the City Center

新颜
New Look

位于广州市中心的地标——广州塔，别名“小蛮腰”，彰显岭南文化的特质——外柔内刚，刚柔并济。她面向的是广州新中轴线和珠江，前者是改革开放的发展硕果、经济腾飞的历史见证，后者是广州文化的发祥源泉，柔和灵动的珠江水系滋养着这片土地，带来了外来文化的熏陶，彰显着城市的柔美与温良。

登塔远眺，城央鳞次栉比的建筑群透着刚毅和冷峻，每一盏灯火中却显露柔情与温暖。游船江上，珠江两岸璀璨灯火细说广州缘何因水而兴，因水而美。快与慢，冷与暖，皆是这座时尚之都的本来面目。

A landmark at the city center, the Canton Tower, alias "the Slender Waist", symolizes the characteristic of Lingnan culture em-dash gentle on the outside and strong on the inside. It faces the new central axis of Guangzhou and the Pearl River, the former being the fruit of the reform and opening up and the witness of the economic take-off, while the latter is the origin of Guangzhou culture. The Pearl River nourishes this land, bringing in other cultures and demonstrating the inclusiveness of the city.

From the top of the tower, one can see that the buildings lined up in the center of the city are hard and cold, but all lights are soft and warm. The bright lights on both sides of the Pearl River tell the story of how Guangzhou grows and prospers along the river. Fast and slow, cold and warm, all elements co-exist in this fashion capital.

花城广州，四季皆有花的相伴。在云雾和凤凰花的映衬下，广州塔变得娇羞朦胧，透露出独有的岭南雅韵。

Guangzhou, the city of flowers, is surrounded by blossoms in all seasons. Amid clouds, mist and phoenix flowers, the Canton Tower looks shy and mysterious with its unique Lingnan elegance.

广州·海珠 / 广州塔

Guangzhou · Haizhu / Canton Tower

广州塔阿尔法探索乐园，全国首个高塔探险乐园，拥有全世界最先进、最安全的高空绳索体验产品。

整个乐园位于广州塔168—330米空间，拥有云端漫步与凌空探险两大核心项目，在这里，不仅能够感受到挑战潜能、超越自我的非凡高空体验，更能以前所未有的独特视界俯瞰羊城。

广州塔阿尔法探索乐园作为广州文旅体融合创新发展的重大项目，为广州塔成为全国文旅行业高质量发展的标杆和典范增添活力，为广州实现老城市新活力做出贡献，为广州文化产业大发展增添新动力。

Canton Tower Landmark α, the first high-tower adventure park in China, has the most advanced and safest high-altitude rope course activities in the world.

The whole park is located at the space between 168 and 330 meters of Canton Tower. It has two major projects: Skywalk and Rope Course. Here, you can not only have the extraordinary experience of challenging your limits, but also overlook the city with an unprecedentedly unique vision.

Canton Tower Landmark α, as a major project for the integration and development of Guangzhou's cultural tourism and sports industry, helps Canton Tower become a role-model for the high-quality development of the national cultural tourism industry, inputs new vitality to the ancient city of Guangzhou, and contributes to the development of cultural industry of Guangzhou.

广州·天河 / 珠江新城

Guangzhou · Tianhe / Zhujiang New Town

珠江新城是广州CBD的核心区域。

Zhujiang New Town is the core area of the CBD of Guangzhou.

新颜
New Look
IMP

广州·越秀 / 近代广州城市中轴线

Guangzhou · Yuexiu / Central Axis of Modern Guangzhou

一座城市的发展足迹，往往铭刻于城市轴线。北起越秀山中山纪念碑，南至海珠广场，这是近代广州城市中轴线，这里铺陈着千年商都的文化脉络。

The development footprints of a city are often inscribed on its axis. From the Zhongshan Monument on Yuexiu Mountain in the north to the Haizhu Square in the south lies the Central Axis of Modern Guangzhou city which lays out the cultural lineage of this thousand-year-old commercial capital.

广州·天河 / 广州新中轴线

Guangzhou · Tianhe / Central Axis of Contemporary Guangzhou

随着广州亚运会的举办，广州新中轴线登上历史舞台，其南段以“岭南特色，花城绿轴”为主题，彰显出现代化都市的蓬勃生机。

With the hosting of the Guangzhou Asian Games, The Central Axis of Contemporary Guangzhou took shape, with its southern section themed on "Lingnan characteristics, Green Axis of the Flower City", highlighting the vigor of this modern metropolis.

新颜

New Look

广州·天河 / 海心桥

Guangzhou · Tianhe / Haixin Bridge

2021年6月25日，横跨珠江的人行景观桥——海心桥正式开通，广州又多了一处“网红”打卡圣地。

On June 25, 2021, The Haixin Bridge, a pedestrian bridge across the Pearl River, was officially opened, adding another internet-famous attraction in Guangzhou.

广州·天河 / 天河商圈

Guangzhou · Tianhe / Tianhe Business Circle

广州·海珠 / 珠江琶醍啤酒文化创意艺术区

Guangzhou · Haizhu / Zhujiang Party Pier Beer Culture and Art Zone

广州·天河 / 珠江新城CBD

Guangzhou · Tianhe / Zhujiang New Town CBD

珠江新城CBD，作为中国三大国家级中央商务区之一、华南地区最大的CBD，是中国300米以上摩天建筑最密集的地方，也是广州市总部经济最为密集的区域。

Zhujiang New Town CBD, as one of the three national central business districts and the largest of its kind in South China, is the densest area with skyscrapers over 300 meters, and the most concentrated area of headquarters economy in Guangzhou.

新颜
New
Look

“绣花”功夫

Meticulous Work

新颜
New Look

未识广州，先闻西关。如今的西关老街，因新景而圈粉无数。

位于恩宁路上的永庆坊，已然成为一处名副其实的网红打卡地，咖啡店、文创店、民宿等新业态吸引不少年轻游客。年轻人纷至沓来，老西关透着青春之气。

以永庆坊为标志的广州市荔湾区恩宁路历史文化街区，在老城微改造的精雕细琢中，以“绣花”功夫，传承文明、延续文化，焕发新活力。

People have often heard about Xiguan before they know Guangzhou. Nowadays, the old Xiguan streets have attracted numerous fans with its new attractions.

Yong Qing Fang on En Ning Road has become a veritable social media sensation, attracting many young visitors with new types of business such as cafes, creative shops and private lodgings. The old Xiguan is filled with youthful vigor.

The En Ning Road Historical and Cultural Site in Liwan District, marked by Yong Qing Fang , refined and revived through the micro-renovation of the old city project, is passing on civilization, extending culture and exuding new vitality.

獵德

广州·天河 / 猎德

Guangzhou · Tianhe / Liede

作为广州首个整体改造的城中村，猎德经历了从农村到新型社区的转变。

As the first urban village in Guangzhou to be transformed as a whole, Liede has undergone a transformation from farmland to a modern community.

广州·荔湾 / 永庆坊

Guangzhou · Liwan / Yong Qing Fang

以永庆坊为标志的广州市荔湾区恩宁路历史文化街区，在老城微改造的精雕细琢中，传承文明、延续文化，焕发出新的活力。

The En Ning Road Historical and Cultural Site in Liwan District, marked by Yong Qing Fang , refined and revived through the micro-renovation of the old city project, is passing on civilization, extending culture and exuding new vitality.

永庆坊微改造之所以成功，在于修旧如旧，建新如故，一边进行原样修复，一边进行改造提升，既保留了岭南建筑的整体风貌和空间肌理，亦更新了配套设施、改善了人居环境。

The success of the micro-renovation of Yong Qing Fang lies in the approach to retaining the old looks of everything through repair, and adopting the old style in new constructions so that restoration and renovation go hand in hand to preserve the overall style and spatial texture of the Lingnan architecture while upgrading the supporting facilities and improving the living environment.

西关大屋是岭南特色传统民居，形成于清朝同治、光绪年间的“西关角”。

满洲窗是西关大屋最富特色的标志之一，窗格用众多五光十色的玻璃镶嵌而成，典雅秀丽，工序十分复杂繁琐。

Xiguan Mansion is a kind of traditional residence of Lingnan built in the Xiguan Corner during the Tongzhi and Guangxu reigns of the Qing Dynasty.

One of the most distinctive features of the Xiguan Mansion is the Manchurian Window. Inlaid with many pieces of colorful glass, this brilliant artifact requires extremely complex manual working procedures.

恩宁路骑楼街

Qilou Street on En Ning Road

恩宁路骑楼街诞生于1931年，周边有李小龙祖居、詹天佑纪念馆、八和会馆、銮舆堂、宝庆大押等具有岭南特色的历史建筑。

Built in 1931, the Qilou street on En Ning Road hosts historical buildings with Lingnan characteristics, such as Bruce Lee's ancestral home, Zhan Tianyou Memorial Hall, the Barwo Guild House, Luan Yu Hall, and Bao Qing Pawnshop.

广州·番禺 / 沙湾古镇

Guangzhou · Panyu / Shawan Ancient Town

沙湾古镇，中国历史文化名镇、广东省旅游特色（狮舞、飘色）镇，是番禺乃至珠三角一带文化古镇的体现，为广东音乐的发源地。

Shawan Ancient Town, a Famous Historical and Cultural Town of China and a Town of Tourist Characteristics (lion dance and Piao Se) of Guangdong Province, is the representative of the ancient cultural town in Panyu and the Pearl River Delta and the birthplace of Cantonese music.

广州·荔湾 / 粤剧艺术博物馆

Guangzhou · Liwan / Cantonese Opera Art Museum

粤剧艺术博物馆以保护、传承、弘扬粤剧艺术为主旨，通过陈列展览、舞台演出、文化交流、教育服务等方式，向公众展示粤剧艺术的精髓和魅力。

Dedicated to the preservation, inheritance and promotion of the art of Cantonese Opera, the Cantonese Opera Art Museum showcases the essence and charm of Cantonese Opera to the public through exhibitions, performances, cultural exchanges and educational services.

城市“绿心”

The "Green Heart" of the City

海珠湿地，地处广州中心城区，是中国特大城市中心规模最大、保存最完整的生态绿核，被誉为广州“绿心”。她因持续产生生态、经济与社会效益，被视为中国生态文明建设和粤港澳大湾区城市可持续发展的窗口。

广东是全国湿地大省，湿地总面积为175.34万公顷，占全省国土面积9.76%，是全国湿地类型最丰富的省份之一。“十三五”期间，省内国家湿地公园年游客人数达2300万人次，带动区域经济发展总量约17亿元。

Located in the heart of Guangzhou, Haizhu wetland is the largest and best-preserved wetland in the center of a mega-city in China, and is known as the "green heart" of Guangzhou. It is regarded as a window into China's ecological preservation and the sustainable development of the cities in the Guangdong-Hong Kong-Macao Greater Bay Area because of the ecological, economic and social benefits it continues to generate.

Guangdong is a major wetland province and one of the provinces with the most diverse wetland types in China, with a total wetland area of 1,753,400 hectares accounting for 9.76% of the its land area. During the 13th Five-Year Plan period, wetland parks in Guangdong had recorded 23 million visits, contributing about 1.7 billion yuan to the regional economic aggregate.

广州·天河 / 海心沙亚运公园

Guangzhou · Tianhe / Haixinsha Asian Games Park

广州海心沙亚运公园位于城市新中轴线花城广场南面，观众座席超2.6万个，能呈现多种艺术表现形式，是广州的重要城市地标和户外大型活动场地。

Guangzhou Haixinsha Asian Games Park is located in the south of Huacheng Square, With more than 26,000 audience seats, it can present various forms of artistic expression. It is an important urban landmark and a venue for large-scale outdoor event in Guangzhou.

广州·越秀 / 麓湖公园

Guangzhou · Yuexiu / Luhu Park

麓湖公园，虽是老牌公园，但焕发出新的光彩。姿态万千、争奇斗艳的四季花海，山环水绕、绿树成荫的风景长廊。

Luhu Park, although an old park, has taken on a new look. The dazzling all-season flower sea and the promenade of lush trees are surrounded by hills.

广州·天河 / 华南国家植物园

Guangzhou · Tianhe / South China Botanical Garden

广州·海珠 / 海珠湿地

Guangzhou · Haizhu / Haizhu Wetland

“海花蛮草连冬有，行处无家不满园。”站在海珠湿地眺望，更能领略唐代诗人张籍笔下广州的意境。

"The sea of flowers and grasses are there even in winter; everywhere you be, no home does not have a full garden." Looking afar from the Haizhu Wetland, one can fully appreciate the mood of Guangzhou in the words of the Tang poet Zhang Ji.

3月的广州街头，像铺上了两条黄色风铃木彩带，在蓝天的映衬下显得格外鲜艳。

The streets of Guangzhou in March are decorated with two ribbons of Tabebuia chrysantha, which look especially bright against the blue sky.

广州·荔湾 / 荔湾湖

Guangzhou · Liwan / Liwan Lake

荔湾湖水上花市，令千年公园焕新颜。

The flower market on the Liwan Lake gives a new look to the thousand-year-old park.

广州·白云 / 白云湖

Guangzhou · Baiyun / Baiyun lake

白云湖位于广东省广州市白云区，是城市绿心，也是广州市最大的人工湖。白云湖集水资源、水生态、水环境、水管理、水经济、水文化于一体，同时兼具防洪减灾、旅游休憩等多项功能，已成为白云湖数字科技城的生态核心。

Baiyun Lake, located in Baiyun District, Guangzhou City, Guangdong Province, is the green heart of the city and the largest artificial lake in Guangzhou. Baiyun Lake integrates water resources, water ecology, water environment, water management, water economy and water culture, as well as multiple functions such as flood control and disaster reduction, tourism and rest, and has become the ecological core of Baiyun Lake Digital Science and Technology City.

广州·荔湾 / 沙面

Guangzhou · Liwan / Shamian

沙面岛上生机盎然的古树与各色异国风情建筑融为一体。

The lush old trees on the Shamian Island and the architecture in various styles blend with each other.

新颜

New Look

新颜

New Look

广州·天河 / 火炉山森林公园
Guangzhou · Tianhe / Huolu Mountain Forest Park

乐游珠江

新声

New Sounds

新彩广州

RENEWED
CHARM
OF
GUANGZHOU

PLEASANT CANTONESE MELODY SURROUNDS BAIYUN MOUNTAIN AND THE PEARL RIVER

Having greenery and scenery out of the window is especially precious in the hustle and bustle of a first-tier city.

When the first ray of the morning wakes up Guangzhou, you can hear the sounds of this livable city.

From Baiyun Mountain to the city's wetland, from campus to the countryside, cicadas' noise echoes in the forest, birds' song rings in the serene mountain. In the early morning, after morning exercise, Guangzhou people come out of the park, enter the restaurant, order a few pieces of dim sum and read the newspaper em-dash such is the most familiar daily routine of them. The sound of two fingers tapping on the table is not only a ritualistic expression, but also a unique cultural symbol of Guangzhou.

Calling all female "pretty woman" and the courtesy words "excuse me" reflect the kindness and modesty of the Cantonese language. "Draping branches and plump fruits hold the message of spring. Separated by mountains and water, hearts still linked." "Ode to the Lychee" is a song for the delicious fruit of Lingnan, and a typical example of the fine sentiments of Cantonese opera.

Both nature's voices and the songs of Cantonese Opera are the sounds of Guangzhou.

云山珠水聚灵气
芬芳粤韵显风华

推窗见绿，出门见景，在繁华喧嚣的一线城市，尤显可贵。

在云山珠水的庇护下，广州从清晨的第一缕阳光中苏醒。只要你是一位耐心的听众，便能倾听到来自这座宜居城市的灵动之声。

蝉噪林逾静，鸟鸣山更幽。从白云山间到城中湿地，从校园到郊野，鸣禽信步，群鸟齐飞，生趣盎然。清晨，结束了晨练的老广从公园而出，上茶楼点上“一盅两件”，翻看报纸，这是广州人最熟悉的日常。两指叩响桌面的声音，不仅是一种充满仪式的表达，更是广州独具特色的文化符号。

一句“靓女”的称呼，一声“唔该”的谦语，是粤语温良谦逊的本意，“枝垂锦弹含春意，隔山隔水，心连心”，一曲《荔枝颂》寄情于岭南佳果，唱出粤剧绵长情意。

从自然灵气到粤韵风华，且听，这是广州的声音。

山水和鸣

Harmony between Mountains and Water

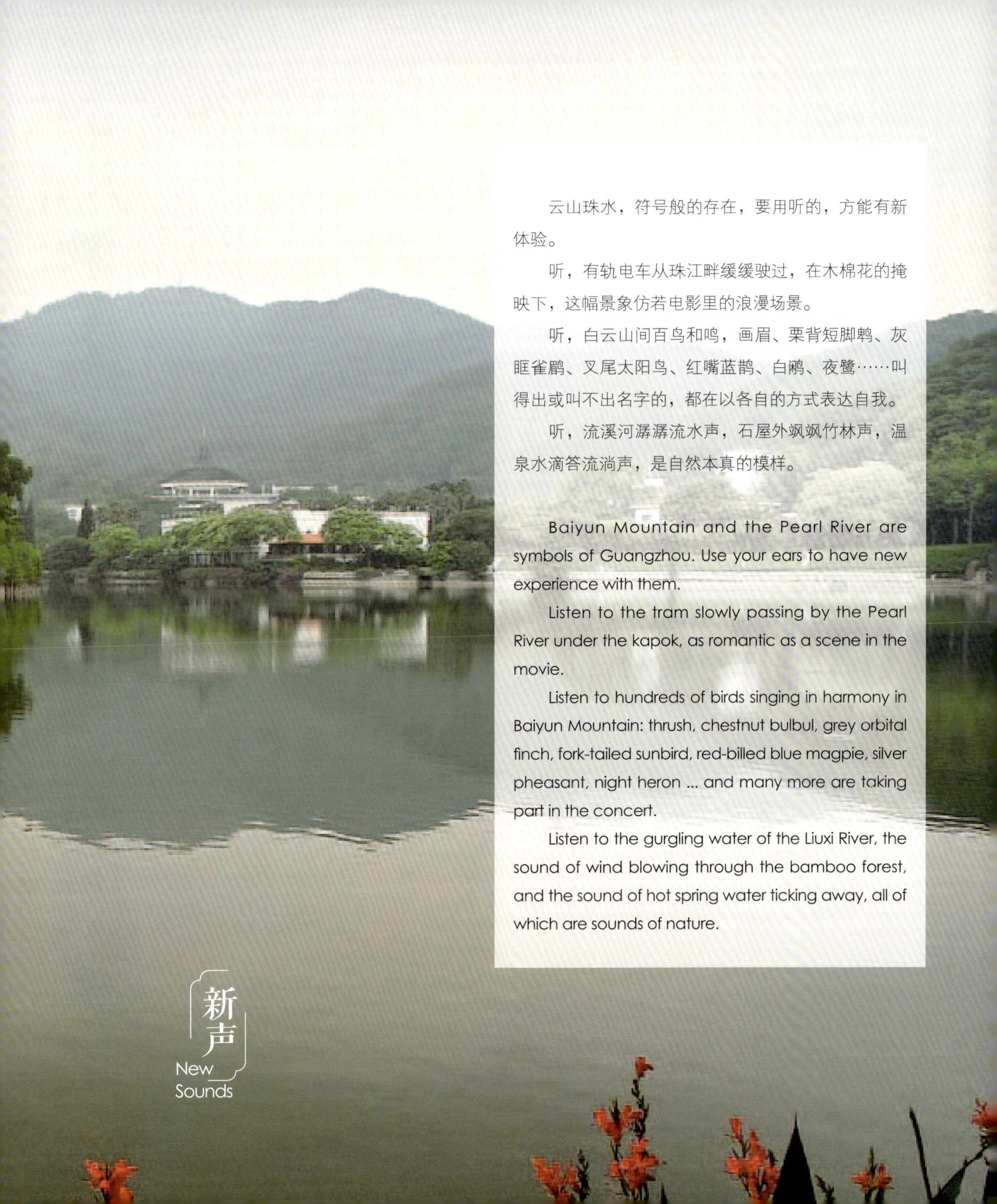

云山珠水，符号般的存在，要用听的，方能有新体验。

听，有轨电车从珠江畔缓缓驶过，在木棉花的掩映下，这幅景象仿若电影里的浪漫场景。

听，白云山间百鸟和鸣，画眉、栗背短脚鹎、灰眶雀鹛、叉尾太阳鸟、红嘴蓝鹊、白鹇、夜鹭……叫得出或叫不出名字的，都在以各自的方式表达自我。

听，流溪河潺潺流水声，石屋外飒飒竹林声，温泉水滴答流淌声，是自然本真的模样。

Baiyun Mountain and the Pearl River are symbols of Guangzhou. Use your ears to have new experience with them.

Listen to the tram slowly passing by the Pearl River under the kapok, as romantic as a scene in the movie.

Listen to hundreds of birds singing in harmony in Baiyun Mountain: thrush, chestnut bulbul, grey orbital finch, fork-tailed sunbird, red-billed blue magpie, silver pheasant, night heron ... and many more are taking part in the concert.

Listen to the gurgling water of the Liuxi River, the sound of wind blowing through the bamboo forest, and the sound of hot spring water ticking away, all of which are sounds of nature.

新声 New Sounds

广州·白云 / 白云山

Guangzhou · Baiyun / Baiyun Mountain

白云山为南粤名山，自古有“羊城第一秀”之称，由30多座山峰组成，是广东最高峰九连山的支脉。广州市白云山风景名胜区是国家5A级旅游景区和国家级风景名胜区。

Baiyun Mountain is a famous mountain in southern Guangdong, known as "the most picturesque site of the Ram City" since ancient times. Consisting of more than 30 peaks, it is a branch range of Guangdong's highest peak, Jiulian Mountain. The Guangzhou Baiyun Mountain Scenic Area is a national 5A-class tourist attraction and a national scenic spot.

广州·增城 / 白水寨

Guangzhou · Zengcheng / Baishuizhai

白水寨，被誉为北回归线上的瑰丽翡翠，拥有原始森林、浅滩湿地、峡谷天池等广东罕见自然生态资源，其中最令人瞩目的当属落差高达428.5米的瀑布——白水仙瀑。

Baishuizhai, known as the emerald on the Tropic of Cancer, is endowed with primitive forests, shoals and wetlands, canyons and lakes and other rare natural resources in Guangdong, the most remarkable of which is the Baishui Fall, a waterfall with a drop of 428.5 meters.

◀ 广州·番禺 / 莲花山

Guangzhou · Panyu / Lotus Mountain

翩跹于水上的鸟儿，是自然的精灵，亦是镜头中的舞者。在广州，多样的自然生态环境，孕育了丰富的鸟类资源。公开数据显示，广州野生鸟类达307种。

The birds fluttering on the water are nature's spirits and dancers for camera. Guangzhou's diverse natural and ecological environment nurtures a rich variety of birds, including 307 species of wild birds.

南沙湿地
Nansha Wetland

广州·花都 / 芙蓉旅游度假区

Guangzhou · Huadu / Furong Tourism Resort

广州·从化 / 石门国家森林公园

Guangzhou · Conghua / Shimen National Forest Park

石门公园碧水环抱，绿岛如茵，是集自然景观、人文景观、森林保健功能于一体的生态型森林公园。其著名的花海景观，营造出如梦如幻的意境。

Surrounded by blue water and decorated by green islands, the Shimen Park is an eco-friendly forest park combining natural and humanistic landscapes and forest healthcare function. Its famous flower sea creates a dream-like atmosphere.

粤音袅袅

Enchanting Cantonese Music

岭南历来是音乐热土，这使岭南音乐既有厚重坚实的历史底蕴，更有涌动不竭的生命活力。从何博众的《雨打芭蕉》，到何柳堂的《赛龙夺锦》，再到吕文成等人创作的《平湖秋月》《步步高》等，一首首家喻户晓的名曲成为经典。

传统走向创新才更具生命力。抗疫期间，广东粤剧院一曲《抗疫有我哋》全网刷屏，“粤剧+饶舌”的演唱形式别具一格，充满力量。

Lingnan has always been a hotbed of music, having a profound historical heritage and an inexhaustible vitality. From He Bozhong's "Raindrops Drummed against the Banana Leaves", to He Liutang's "Dragon Boat Racing", and "Autumn Moon over the Placid Lake" and "Rising Higher with Every Step" composed by Lü Wencheng and others, many household music pieces come from here.

Tradition is only more long-lasting with innovation. During the pandemic, "We are Here to Fight the Pandemic", a song by Guangdong Cantonese Opera Institute has been a hit on the internet with its creative and powerful "Cantonese Opera + rap" style.

广州·天河 / 广州大剧院

Guangzhou · Tianhe / Guangzhou Opera House

广州大剧院坐落于广州珠江新城，由广州市政府投资建设，历时5年建造完成。著名建筑设计师扎哈·哈迪德和声学大师哈罗德·马歇尔爵士联袂设计，使其获得“世界十大歌剧院”（《今日美国》评）、“世界最壮观剧院”（英国《每日电讯》评）等国际赞誉。

Located in Zhujiang New Town, Guangzhou Opera House was invested by Guangzhou municipal government and was built for 5 years. It was designed by famed architect Zaha Hadid and acoustician Sir Harold Marshall, and has won international accolades such as one of the "10 best opera houses around the world" (*USA Today*) and the "world's most spectacular theatre" (*The Telegraph*).

粤剧，正在从剧院舞台走向大众生活。广州市荔湾湖公园内粤剧迷们观看表演。

Cantonese Opera is brought from the theatre stage to people's everyday life. Fans of Cantonese Opera were watching a performance in the Liwan Lake Park, Guangzhou.

大型新编历史粤剧《文成公主》在广州大剧院公演。

The large-scale new historical Cantonese opera *Princess Wencheng* was performed at the Guangzhou Opera House.

广州·番禺 / 长隆野生动物园

Guangzhou · Panyu / Chimelong Safari Park

广州·越秀 / 广州动物园

Guangzhou · Yuexiu / Guangzhou Zoo

广州·番禺 / 宝墨园水上飘色

Guangzhou · Panyu / The colorful performance on the water of the Baomo Garden

广州·番禺 / 宝墨园·汉服秀

Guangzhou · Panyu / Hanfu Show in the Baomo Garden

广州·从化 / 中国国家版本馆广州分馆

Guangzhou · Conghua / The Guangzhou branch of the China National Archives of Publications and Culture

中国国家版本馆广州分馆建筑群以“中华典藏、岭南山水、时代新韵、文明灯塔”为总体构思，充分体现了人文、地域、自然与时代的融合统一，打造了传世经典的中华文化殿堂形象。

The building complex of the Guangzhou branch of the China National Archives of Publications and Culture is designed with the concept of "Chinese collections, Lingnan landscapes, new charm of the times, and lighthouse of civilization", which fully embodies the integration of humanity, region, nature and the times, creating a classic image of Chinese culture.

听见烟火

The Sound of Tradition and Modernity

珠江水，是浸润广州人心田的养料。水丰沛了文明，滋润了生活，广州的民俗文化依水而生。

端午到，扒龙舟，是广州最具辨识度的民俗活动之一，亦是广州人的集体记忆。随着鼓声逼近，扒龙舟的热闹更为真切。

新年到，舞醒狮，是广州人迎接喜事的重要仪式之一。锣鼓声中，醒狮忽而辗转腾挪、欢腾跳跃，忽而摇头摆尾、低眉颔首，妙趣横生。

波罗诞、沙湾飘色等岭南最具代表性的民间活动，热闹非凡。

在广州，不仅能“听见传统”，更能“听见现代”。广州是潮流文化的重镇，游戏、街舞、滑板、赛车……所有年轻人喜欢的生活方式正在融入到这座古老城市的肌理中。

The Pearl River has been enriching the civilization of Guangzhou and nourishing people's life. Guangzhou's folk culture is based on water.

Dragon boat racing on the Dragon Boat Festival is one of the most recognizable folk customs in Guangzhou and the sound of approaching drums is a collective memory of Guangzhou people.

Lion dance is one of the most important rituals for Guangzhou people to usher in the Chinese New Year. With the sound of drums and gongs, the lion suddenly moves around and jumps for joy, while at other times it wags its tail and lowers its eyebrows, bringing in endless fun.

Boluodan Temple Fair, Shawan Piaose parade and other most representative folk events of Lingnan are also vibrant and exciting.

In Guangzhou, you hear not only the tradition, but also the modernity. Guangzhou is a center of trendy culture, where computer games, street dancing, skateboarding, Car racing and other favorites of young people gather.

广州 / 醒狮

Guangzhou / Lion Dance

醒狮是融武术、舞蹈、音乐等为一体的文化活动。自古以来，广东醒狮被认为是驱邪避害的吉祥瑞物，每逢节庆，或有重大活动，必有醒狮助兴，长盛不衰，历代相传。

The lion dance is a cultural activity that combines martial arts, dance and music. Since ancient times, the lion dance has been regarded as an auspicious thing to ward off evil spirits. in Guangdong, so it has always been performed during festivals and major events, and has been passed down from generation to generation.

广州·海珠 / 广州国际龙舟邀请赛

Guangzhou · Haizhu / Guangzhou International Dragon Boat Invitational Competition

广州·海珠 / 太古仓码头

Guangzhou · Haizhu / Taigucang Wharf

太古仓被年轻人视为广州“元老级”网红打卡地，亦是广州“夜经济”的发源地之一。

Taigucang Wharf is one of the young people's must-go internet-famous sites in Guangzhou and a cradle of Guangzhou's "night economy".

广州·越秀 / 珠江夜游

Guangzhou · Yuexiu / Pearl River Night Cruise

珠江夜游是广州夜间旅游的金字招牌之一。

The Pearl River Night Cruise has become one of the representative nightlife activities in Guangzhou.

广州·番禺 / 长隆飞鸟乐园

Guangzhou · Panyu / Chimelong Birds Park

长隆飞鸟乐园，荟萃世界各地珍稀鸟类三百多种，一万多只鸟类自然栖息，是一个集鸟类观赏和科普教育于一体的湿地生态主题公园。

Chimelong Birds Park is a wetland park that integrates bird watching and science education, gathering more than 300 species of rare birds from all over the world, and more than 10,000 birds inhabit here.

广州·番禺 / 长隆水上世界

Guangzhou · Panyu / Chimelong Water Park

长隆水上世界堪称全年游客总数排名世界第一的水上乐园，园区拥有众多世界金奖游乐设施，打造过诸多影响力“出圈”的水上派对。

Chimelong Water Park is the world's number one water park in terms of the number of annual visitors, with amusement facilities that has won many world-class awards, and has held many phenomenal water parties.

广州马拉松赛

Guangzhou Marathon

广州·天河 / 天河体育中心

Guangzhou · Tianhe / Tianhe Sports Center

体育场馆，是一届大型赛事为举办地留下的最直观财富。六运会时建设的广州天河体育中心，如今身处城市新中轴线上，记录着这座城市那些狂欢、沸腾的片刻。

Sports venues are the most direct legacy of major sport events. Guangzhou Tianhe Sports Center, built for the sixth National Games, now sits on the city's new axis, recording those moments of revelry and passion in Guangzhou.

南国的梦

Dream of the South

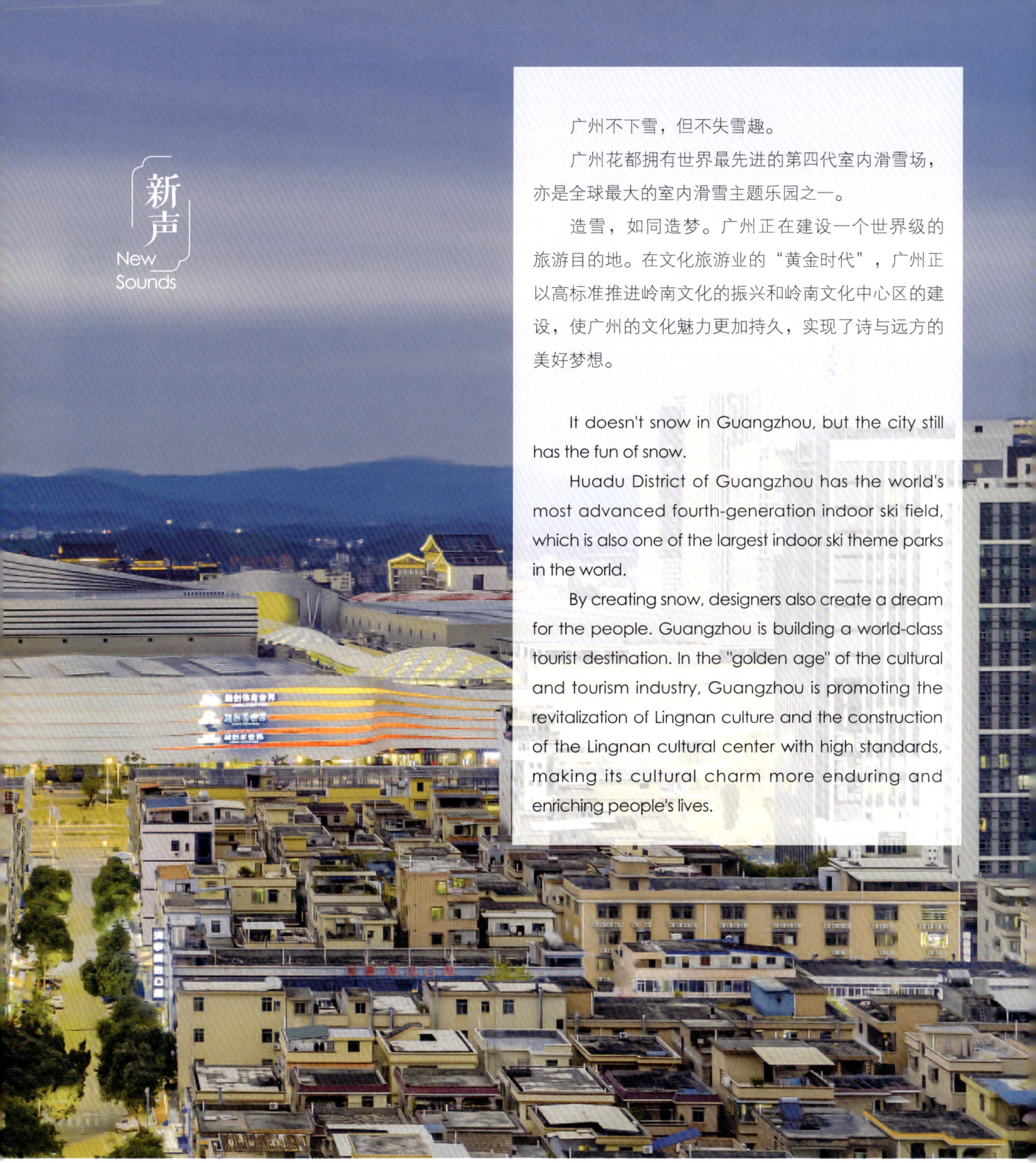

广州不下雪，但不失雪趣。

广州花都拥有世界最先进的第四代室内滑雪场，亦是全球最大的室内滑雪主题乐园之一。

造雪，如同造梦。广州正在建设一个世界级的旅游目的地。在文化旅游业的“黄金时代”，广州正以高标准推进岭南文化的振兴和岭南文化中心区的建设，使广州的文化魅力更加持久，实现了诗与远方的美好梦想。

It doesn't snow in Guangzhou, but the city still has the fun of snow.

Huadu District of Guangzhou has the world's most advanced fourth-generation indoor ski field, which is also one of the largest indoor ski theme parks in the world.

By creating snow, designers also create a dream for the people. Guangzhou is building a world-class tourist destination. In the "golden age" of the cultural and tourism industry, Guangzhou is promoting the revitalization of Lingnan culture and the construction of the Lingnan cultural center with high standards, making its cultural charm more enduring and enriching people's lives.

广州·花都 / 室内滑雪场

Guangzhou · Huadu / Indoor Ski Field

在华南最大室内滑雪场，年轻人尽情体验滑雪的乐趣。

Young people are enjoying the fun of skiing in the largest indoor ski field in South China.

广州·从化 / 美丽乡村稻草节

Guangzhou · Conghua / Guangzhou Xitang Rice Straw Festival

广州 · 番禺 / 长隆国际大马戏

Guangzhou · Panyu / Chimelong International Circus

广州·海珠 / 广州艺术博物院（广州美术馆）新馆

Guangzhou · Haizhu / The New Guangzhou Museum of Art

广州艺术博物院（广州美术馆）新馆似“水中盛放的英雄花”。

The new Guangzhou Museum of Art is like a Kapok flower on the water.

广州·海珠 / 广州数字纪实视听产业园

Guangzhou · Haizhu / Guangzhou Digital Documentary Audio-Visual Industrial Park

广州数字纪实视听产业园（简称“豆园DOC.PARK”），是全国首家以纪实内容为主体的产业园区，致力于服务内容产业，专注打造内容生态，带动产业系统升级，推动数字纪实视听产业的国际合作与传播。

Guangzhou Digital Documentary Audio-Visual Industrial Park (DOC. PARK) is the first industrial park in China focusing on nonfiction content. It is committed to serving the content industry, creating a content ecosystem, driving industrial upgrading, and promoting international cooperation and communication of the digital documentary audio-visual industry.

广州·海珠 / 数字虚拟人

Guangzhou · Haizhu / Digital Virtual Characters

海珠区首批数字虚拟人，5位数字居民分别是：

001号数字居民、海珠区数字文创产业代言人、海珠发布形象IP　G仔

002号咏声动漫数字虚拟人　西汐

003号粤传媒数字虚拟人　岳古今

004号三七互娱数字虚拟人　葱妹

005号映宇宙集团数字虚拟人　映映

The first group of digital virtual characters in Haizhu district. These five digital residents are:
001 digital resident, spokesperson for the digital cultural and creative industry of Haizhu district, and the image IP of Haizhu Release: Gzai
002 Winsing Animation Digital Virtual Character: Cici
003 Canton Media Digital Virtual Character: Yue Gu Jin
004 37 Interactive Entertainment Digital Virtual Character: Cong Mei
005 Inkeverse Group Digital Virtual Character: Yingying

蓮香樓
蓮香樓
蓮香樓

新味

New Tastes

新彩广州

RENEWED
CHARM
OF
GUANGZHOU

INHERITING CUISINE TRADITIONS AND INFUSING WISDOM INTO THE THREE MEALS OF THE DAY

Guangzhou, home of Cantonese cuisine, has a long and enduring food culture.

"Dare to be the first in the world" is the culinary wisdom of the people of Guangzhou. Being away from the center of the country historically gave inclusiveness to Cantonese cuisine culture. From ancient times to the present day, Guangzhou people take everyday life seriously and dedicate their wisdom to the meals, making the most of what they have, experimenting boldly, pushing the boundaries and passing on the artisanal skills.

In addition to Guangzhou people's unchanging belief in food, the growing number of business types of the catering industry has provided more possibilities to this gourmet paradise. Although the Canton style sidewalk snack booth has rolled out across the country, food shops unique to Guangzhou or emerging here, such as Cantonese dessert shops and milk tea shops, continue to fill in the gaps beyond the formal meals, and have become must-go spots and social centers for online celebrities.

As Guangzhou has become a first-tier city in the world, its dining options become more international. From the settlement of the Bocuse d'Or in Guangzhou to the arrival of the Michelin Guide, from the going out of local Cantonese cuisine to the introduction of international cuisine, Guangzhou's food culture has once again shown its inclusiveness and diversity.

匠心传承真滋味
一日三餐凝智慧

粤菜之乡广州，饮食文化悠久，且历久弥新。

敢为天下先，是广州人的饮食智慧。粤菜文化的包容性源于偏于一隅的地缘文化，由古至今，广州人敬畏生活，把日子捧在手里过，一日三餐凝聚了生活的智慧，物尽其用，大胆尝试，推陈出新，匠心传承。

在广州人对“食”不变的信念之外，饮食业日趋丰富的业态，为“美食天堂”提供了充足的养料。尽管广式大排档已经推向全国各地，但糖水店、奶茶店一类广州独有或兴起的店铺，仍一直孜孜不倦地填补着正餐以外的空白，不动声色地成为“网红”簇拥的打卡地和社交场。

跻身世界一线城市，广州的餐饮格局亦更国际化。从博古斯世界烹饪大赛落户广州，到米其林榜单入穗，从本土粤菜“走出去”到国际佳肴“引进来”，广州饮食文化再次展现其兼容并包、海纳百川的特质。

敢为人先
Daring to be the First

“头啖汤”，广东俗话，意为第一拨出锅的汤，味道最鲜。敢饮“头啖汤”，被视为广东人敢为人先的写照。

这句俗语亦与粤人喝汤的饮食习惯密切相关。先上汤，再上菜，这是广州人宴席中的老规矩，一口暖汤，滋润心田。

广州饮食市场的蓬发，亦得益于改革开放的“头啖汤”。改革开放以来，在饮食多样化方面，几乎没有哪个城市能与广州抗衡。“十步一酒楼，五步一茶室”，数十年来成为广州餐饮蓬勃发展最直观的缩影。

建设六马路，簇拥着数百家具有异国特色的餐厅、酒吧、咖啡厅；以北京路为中心，东至越秀桥，南至海珠广场，西至解放路，北至东风路，聚集了大量的广州实力派餐饮企业；上下九步行街，“百步之内必有小吃”，从银记肠粉，到广州酒家、莲香楼，再到陶陶居、南信双皮奶……一街尝尽西关味道；泮塘路的老字号，从泮溪酒家、向群饭店等粤菜餐厅，到利口福、宝生园等手信店，与荔枝湾涌的美景相映成辉。

The Cantonese saying "first sip of soup" means the first bowl of soup that comes out of the pot, which has the freshest taste. Daring to take the first sip of soup is seen as a reflection of the Cantonese people's courage to be the pioneer.

This proverb is also closely related to the Cantonese eating habit of soup. It is a rule on Guangzhou banquet that soup is served first, before other dishes.

The development of Guangzhou's catering market also benefits from the "first sip of soup" of the reform and opening up. Since the reform and opening up, few cities have been able to compete with Guangzhou in terms of culinary diversity. For decades, "one restaurant in ten steps, and one teahouse in five steps" has been the most visual depiction of Guangzhou's culinary boom.

Jianshe Liu Malu is surrounded by hundreds of restaurants, pubs and cafes in different countries' styles; the area with Beijing Road as the center, east to Yuexiu Bridge, south to Haizhu Square, west to Jiefang Road and north to Dongfeng Road, gathers a large number of Guangzhou's major catering enterprises; on the Shang Xia Jiu Pedestrian Street, "within every hundred steps there will be a snack bar", from Yinji Rice Noodle Rolls, to Guangzhou Restaurant, Lian Xiang Lou, Tao Tao Ju and Nan Xin milk custard; on Pan Tang Road, from Cantonese restaurants such as Panxi Restaurant and Xiang Qun Restaurant, to food shops such as Li Kou Fu and Bao Sheng Yuan, the time-honored brands are an inseparable part of the beauty of Lychee Bay Scenic Area.

一盅两件

One Cup and Two Pieces

一盅两件，是广州早茶文化中的典型符号之一，亦是广州人生活中的一部分。饮茶，于广州这座城市而言不仅是一种吃食，也是一种文化，更是一种社交方式。

One Cup and Two Pieces is one of the typical symbols of Guangzhou's morning tea culture and a part of Guangzhou people's life. Drinking tea (eating dim sum) is not only a kind of dining, but also a culture and a way of socializing in this city.

粤菜

Cantonese Cuisine

粤菜“端出”我们美好时代色香味俱全的盛宴佳肴。

The Cantonese cuisine "serves" the feast delicacies of our beautiful times.

广州·海珠 / 石溪龙船饭

Guangzhou · Haizhu / Shixi Dragon Boat Meal

端午吃了龙船饭，接个好彩头，全年事事顺利，龙马精神，风调雨顺，五谷丰登，好运连连。

Cantonese believe that everything will go well throughout the year after having Dragon Boat Meal during Dragon Boat Festival.

广州·荔湾 / 泮溪酒家

Guangzhou · Liwan / Panxi Restaurant

相邻荔枝湾景区河畔的泮溪酒家，位于西关大屋社区建筑群之中，是广州市最具代表的园林酒家之一。

Adjacent to the riverside of the Lychee Bay Scenic Area is the Panxi Restaurant. Located in the Xiguan Mansion community complex, it is one of the most representative garden restaurants in Guangzhou.

广州·荔湾 / 陶陶居

Guangzhou · Liwan / Tao Tao Ju

陶陶居，始创于1880年，是目前广东餐饮界历史最悠久的老字号。她是广府文化的参与者、见证者，被视为一本跨越百年的饮食活字典，生动展现了广州社会发展的变迁史。

Tao Tao Ju, founded in 1880, is the oldest time-honored brand among restaurants in Guangdong. It is a participant and witness of Cantonese culture, and is regarded a living dictionary of food and drink spanning a century, vividly showcasing the history of social changes of Guangzhou.

不时不食

Eating What the Season Offers

《论语》所言“不时，不食”，《黄帝内经》亦说“司岁备物”，指的都是应时令进食的膳食智慧。广州人的饮食哲学延续了这份古老的养生智慧，人们在发掘美味的同时，亦积累了时令饮食的菜谱，这些无论是在高大上的粤菜馆中，抑或在大排档里均有迹可循。

入春，荔枝菌是值得守候的美味佳肴。贵有“岭南菌王”美誉的荔枝菌，生长于每年五六月的荔枝树下，入馔至鲜至美。

“春边秋鲤夏三黎”中的三黎鱼，就是西江盛产的河鲜，鱼肉细嫩、脂肪饱满，烹熟后有异香，配以苦瓜，更显甘香，这是老广们钟情的老味道。

秋天到，新垦莲藕上桌了。肥大丰满、松化无渣、藕香浓郁，足以担当得起“国家地理标志产品”的称号。

冬天里的迟菜心，天气愈冷愈能孕育鲜甜的滋味。在湿冷的广州，一口温暖而鲜甜的迟菜心抵得过一寸阳光。

The Analects of Confucius says "do not eat what is not in season", and the Yellow Emperor's Classic of Internal Medicine says "food is prepared according to the time of the year", both referring to the wisdom of eating what is in season. Guangzhou's food philosophy inherits this ancient wisdom of health and wellness; the recipes for seasonal meals accumulated over generations can be found in both high-class Cantonese restaurants and food stalls.

In spring, lychee mushroom is a delicacy worth waiting for. Known as the "King of Fungi in Lingnan", this kind of mushroom grows under lychee trees in May and June every year and makes the most delicious dish.

"Eat bream in spring, carp in autumn and Sanli in summer." The Sanli fish here is a delicacy of Xijiang River. The fish is tender and fatty, and has an aromatic flavor when cooked; when served with bitter gourd, the mouth-watering taste is Guangzhou people's favorite.

When autumn arrives, Xinken lotus roots are served. The lotus root is plump, soft and dross-free, with a rich lotus aroma that is worthy of the title of National Geographical Indication Product.

The colder the weather is, the sweeter the taste of the Late Choy Sum will be. In the chilly winter of Guangzhou, a bite of the warm and sweet Late Choy Sum dish is like an inch of sunshine.

荔枝虾球

Lychee Shrimp Balls

荔枝虾球是广东名菜之一。荔枝的清新香甜与海产特有的鲜味相互包裹，味道诱人。

Lychee shrimp balls are a famous Cantonese dish. The fresh and sweet taste of lychee is intertwined with the unique freshness of seafood, giving off a tempting aroma.

菜心

Choy Sum

哪怕是普通的菜心，掐头去尾的“菜远”亦格外精致。不时不食，不鲜不食，在蔬菜的烹饪上亦体现出广州人的饮食习惯。

Even ordinary choy sum, could make tasty dish. People in Guangzhou will nip off the head and only keep the tender part which is known as "Caiyuan" before cooking. The cooking of vegetables also reflects the eating habit of Guangzhou people that they only eat what is in season and fresh.

广州·南沙 / 莲藕

Guangzhou · Nansha / Lotus roots

新味

New Tastes

▶

广州·南沙 / 十九涌海鲜

Guangzhou · Nansha / Shi Jiu Chong Seafood

海纳百川

Vast Ocean Admitting Hundreds of Rivers

新味 New Tastes

依海而生的广州，是千年不衰的通商口岸，中西文化在此交汇交融，亦体现在饮食生活中。

外地友人不会因为身处广州而感到陌生，因为这里总是能够找到家乡的味道。

一份广州米其林榜单，集纳了从广州到全国乃至世界各地的风味美食，从豪放的西北风味，到细腻的江南小菜，从琳琅满目的广式点心，到色香俱全的麻辣火锅，从精巧别致的日式料理，到丰俭由人的西餐……

Guangzhou has been a prosperous commerce port for a thousand years. Here Chinese and Western cultures meet and mingle, which is also reflected in its food offering.

Foreigners will not feel unfamiliar in Guangzhou because they can always find a taste of home here.

The Michelin Guide Guangzhou includes flavors from this city to the rest of the country and around the world, from the bold flavors of the northwest to the delicate dishes of the south of the Yangtze River, from an eyeful of Cantonese dim sum to spicy hot pots, from sophisticated Japanese cuisine to Western food sumptuous or simple ...

精致粤味

Delicate Cantonese Flavor

食在广东，潮鲜客香粤精。

粤菜最重原汁原味，清中求鲜，淡中求美，实而不华，以质取胜，博得更多“返寻味”。

粤菜不仅全国开花，更红遍全球，赢得“中国形象大使”美誉。

In Guangdong, the Chaozhou cuisine is fresh, Hakka cuisine is tasty and the Cantonese cuisine is delicate.

Cantonese cuisine emphasizes the original flavor, freshness, light seasoning, and being unadorned. It wins people's heart with the quality and always attracts people to come back.

Cantonese cuisine not only blooms nationwide, but also becomes popular worldwide, earning the reputation of "China's image ambassador".

广州·荔湾 / 白天鹅宾馆·玉堂春暖

Guangzhou · Liwan / Jade River Restaurant, White Swan Hotel

广州市民一早相聚喝早茶。大家边喝茶，边聊天，边品尝广州美食，享受着生活。

Guangzhou citizens get together to have morning tea in a hotel early in the morning. They drink tea, chat, taste Guangzhou food and enjoy life together.

经典广式点心

Classic Cantonese dim sum

五福临门

Five dishes signifying five blessings

四热荤

Four hot dishes

广州·从化 / 流溪河第一湾

Guangzhou · Conghua / The First Bay of Liuxi River

新物

New Items

新彩广州

RENEWED
CHARM
OF
GUANGZHOU

NEW FORM OF CULTURAL AND TOURIST CONSUMPTION

As a national central city, the gateway hub of South China and one of the largest tourism centers of China, Guangzhou is on its way to becoming a world-class tourism destination.

To achieve this goal, the city need to enrich the business forms of the cultural and tourism industry, stimulate cultural and tourist consumption, and build a better space for the hosts and customers to share.

Traditionally, tourism resources are only natural sceneries and cultural monuments. Today, the achievements of economic and social development and an enjoyable leisure life also attract tourists. Through their trips, tourists not only obtain sensual enjoyment, but also increase their love of the country and cultural pride.

In the countryside lodgings, people find artistic style and small blessings; in the cultural exhibitions in the city, people find "poetry and faraway places"; on the cruise ships or gachts at sea, there are dreamers and explorers; in the camps in the countryside, there are fun and warmth of family gathering ...

These new consumption scenarios of cultural tourism are the realization of the proverb "read a thousand books and travel a thousand miles".

文旅消费新业态 主客共享新空间

作为国家中心城市、华南门户枢纽、全国最大的旅游集散地之一，广州正在朝“世界级旅游目的地”的目标进发。

要实现这一目标，需要丰富文旅业态，激活文旅消费，共建主客共享美好空间。

传统意义上的旅游资源，无非山水资源和人文古迹。如今，经济社会发展成就和美好休闲生活均构成了旅游吸引物。游客在行程中不仅关注人间烟火的生活气息，也集聚着家国情怀和文化自豪。

乡村的民宿里，有文艺范和小确幸；城中的文化展览中，有“诗和远方”；海上的邮轮游艇上，有逐梦者和探险家；郊野的房车营地内，有家庭相聚的温暖和亲子互动的乐趣……

这些文旅新消费场景，不仅让“读万卷书、行万里路”有了现实场景，更为美好生活增加了全新的内涵。

乡村民宿，成为寄托乡愁的美丽归处。由有180年历史的客家围屋改造而成的吾乡石屋，由知青学校改造而成的木主题民宿菁木山舍，枕着云海入眠的云山舍，拥有世间香境的溪云香舍，望得见山水的探云田居，一房一景的云水间，大隐于闹市中的艺霖坊陶舍小隐客栈，入选首批广州精品民宿，于美景中创造美意空间，让都市人感受诗意时光。

慢下来，方能体会诗意。水上巴士，予人浪漫的城市观光；万里碧道，承载着休闲生活的美好时光；空中云道，连接着沿路风景；南粤古驿道，延绵着岭南文脉；田园火车，搭载着孩童的童真记忆；房车露营，装载着彩衣娱亲天伦之乐。

The emerging private rural lodgings have become places to relax people's minds and bodies. A 180-year-old Hakka round house was transformed into My Village Stone House; a school over 50 years ago was renovated into the wood-themed lodge Jing Mu Shan She; in Yun Shan She, one sleeps in the cloud sea; in Xi Yun Xiang She, people are immersed in natural fragrance; in Tan Yun Tian Ju, guests enjoy the mountains and water right out of the window; in Yun Shui Jian, each room offers a different view; the Xiaoyin Inn of Yi Lin Fang Ceramic House is a seclusion in the crowded city. They are selected as the first batch of Guangzhou Boutique Private Lodgings for the poetic moments they provide to city dwellers.

Slow down to experience the poetry of life. The water bus provides a romantic city tour; the greenway allows good time of leisure life; the Sky Cloud Route connects sceneries along the way; the South Yue ancient post road extends the cultural lineage of Lingnan; the train in the field carries memories of children; the camp is loaded with the joy of family gathering.

诗意空间

Poetic Space

广州·花都 / 九龙湖旅游度假区

Guangzhou · Huadu / Jiulong Lake Tourist Resort

广州·花都 / 北迹露营一号

Guangzhou · Huadu / Tropic of Cancer Camping Site

广州·从化 / 艾米小镇

Guangzhou · Conghua / Aimi Town

广州·增城 / 吾乡石屋田园度假酒店

Guangzhou · Zengcheng / Wuxiang Stone House Pastoral Resort Hotel

绿道

Greenway

新物

New Items

广州 · 增城 / 荔湖碧道

Guangzhou · Zengcheng / Lihu Lake Ecological Belt

人文时光

Heritage Collection

历史街区，是承载文化之泉的容器。从辟于北宋庆历年间的“广州文化第一街”文德路，到“广州最美老街”恩宁路，从保存完好的清代古建筑群——聚龙村，到“中国民间文化艺术之乡”沙湾古镇，每一处都有一份丰沛的历史养料等待汲取。

粤书吧，集纳诗和远方。在广东粤剧院，粤书吧融入了艺术元素；在广州南沙花园酒店，粤书吧包含着休闲元素。

The historic districts are vessels for the fountain of culture. From Wende Road, the "first cultural street in Guangzhou", which was established during the Qingli period of the Northern Song Dynasty, to En Ning Road "the most beautiful old street in Guangzhou" , from Julong Village, the well-preserved buildings of the Qing Dynasty, to the Shawan Ancient Town, the "hometown of Chinese folk culture and arts", each place is a rich source of historical nourishment.

The Reading Bars carry people's longing for poetry and faraway places. At the Guangdong Cantonese Opera Institute, the Reading Bar incorporates artistic elements; while at the Nansha Garden Hotel, the Reading Bar provides leisure environment.

广州·荔湾 / 恩宁路街区

Guangzhou · Liwan / En Ning Road

广州·越秀 / 广州百年新河浦历史文化街区

Guangzhou · Yuexiu / Century-old Xinhepu Historical and Cultural District in Guangzhou

新物

New Items

广州·荔湾 / 聚龙村

Guangzhou · Liwan / Julong Village

广州·白云 / 神农草堂中医药博物馆

Guangzhou · Baiyun / Shennong Cottage Traditional Chinese Medicine Museum

广州·海珠 / 广州市文化馆

Guangzhou · Haizhu / Guangzhou Cultural & Arts Center

广州·白云 / 广州白云国际会议中心国际会堂
Guangzhou · Baiyun / Baiyun International Conference Center

广州·越秀 / 广州城隍庙

Guangzhou · Yuexiu / Guangzhou City God Temple

广州·越秀 / 西湖花市

Guangzhou · Yuexiu / West Lake Flower Market

向海而进

Towards the Sea

新物 New Items

自古以来，广州就是一座港口型城市。作为中国最早对外开放和从未关闭过的贸易通商口岸，在珠江三角洲航海史、贸易史，乃至世界贸易史上皆占据重要地位。因为港口，广州拥有两千年长盛不衰的历史，因为港口，广州是海上丝绸之路的发祥地，成为对外开放的窗口。

广州从未停止过对外开放的脚步。如今，南沙港已成为中国南部最大的单体港区，广州港口货物吞吐量达全球第五，全球航运枢纽地位日益凸显。

看海，已然不足以体会这座滨海之城的气魄。从游艇码头，到邮轮母港，从近距离观海，到踏海逐浪，再到航海远游，多层次的体验，才能了解广州为何向海而进。

Guangzhou has been a port-oriented city since ancient times. As the first port in China to open to the outside world and an uninterrupted trade and commerce port, Guangzhou has been playing an important role in the maritime and trade history of the Pearl River Delta and even in the trade history of the world. Because of the port, Guangzhou has been prosperous for two thousand years; because of the port, Guangzhou is the birthplace of the Maritime Silk Road and the window open to the outside world.

Guangzhou has never closed its door to the outside world. Today, Nansha Port has become the largest single port area in South China, and the cargo throughput of Guangzhou's ports has reached the fifth largest in the world, making the city an increasingly prominent global shipping hub.

Today what you can do here is far more than looking at the sea. With marinas and the homeport of cruise ship, one can enjoy the sea up close, ride the waves, or sail away, having a variety of experiences.

广州·海珠 / 黄埔古港

Guangzhou · Haizhu / Huangpu Ancient Port

见证了广州“海上丝绸之路”繁荣的黄埔古港，矗立在时间的浩荡长风之中，任凭后来者不断凭吊、重温160多年前的繁华胜景。

The ancient port of Huangpu, which witnessed the prosperity of the Maritime Silk Road in Guangzhou, stands amidst the river of time, allowing people to revisit the hustle and bustle of more than 160 years ago.

广州·黄埔 / 南海神庙

Guangzhou · Huangpu / the Immortal Temple of South Sea

新物
New Items

广州·南沙 / 游艇会

Guangzhou · Nansha / Nansha Marina

2011年，广州南沙游艇会成立，标志着中国内地游艇会正式与国际化高水平游艇会接轨。作为中国大陆首家荣获五金锚奖的游艇会，南沙游艇会为广州帆船运动的发展提供了有力的支持。

In 2011, Nansha Marina was established, marking the alignment of marina in the Chinese mainland with high-level ones internationally. As the first marina in the Chinese mainland to achieve the 5 Gold Anchor Rating, Nansha Marina provides strong support for the development of sailing in Guangzhou.

从“处女星号”到“云顶梦号”再到“新浪漫号”，广州南沙邮轮母港的启用，填补了广州邮轮基础设施空白，标志着广州国际邮轮产业发展步入新阶段。

The opening of the Guangzhou Nansha International Cruise Home Port has filled the gap in Guangzhou's cruise infrastructure and has marked a new stage in the development of Guangzhou's international cruise industry.

新物
New Items

避世田园

Idyll Far from the Crowd

新物 New Items

金色稻田、涓涓溪水、精致民居、如黛青山，这些美丽乡村的必备元素构成了一幅现实图景，散发着浓浓乡愁，承载着家的味道。位于从化的米埗村，地势平坦，土地肥沃，环境优美，乡风淳朴，交通便利。这里的稻田小火车出片率极高，早已远近闻名。

位于增城的莲塘村，村民们念活“山水经”“田园经”，分季节、规模化种植稻田和花海，村庄变身为“秋夏稻谷双丰闻稻香，冬去春来花开逛花海”的网红打卡点。

这些美丽乡村充分利用当地文化资源，运用生态设计理念，改造旧物，物尽其用，最终返璞归真。

With its vast flat land, fertile soil, picturesque surroundings, unsophisticated lifestyle and convenient transportation, Mipu Village in Conghua is a tale of idyll coming true. The picture-perfect sight of the small train on the paddy field here has long been known far and wide.

In Liantang Village of Zengcheng, the villagers grow large areas of rice in summer and autumn, and flowers in winter and spring, making the village a popular tourist spot.

These beautiful villages make full use of local cultural resources and apply ecological design concepts to revive their original beauty.

广州·从化 / 溪头村
Guangzhou · Conghua / Xitou Village

广州·花都 / 红山村

Guangzhou ·Huadu / Hongshan Village

春到红山村，金黄色的油菜花开得喜人。凭借着得天独厚的地理优势以及山清水秀的自然景色，近年来红山村乡村旅游的发展驶入了快车道。

When spring arrives in Hongshan Village, the golden rape flowers are in delightful bloom. With its unique geographical advantage and the natural beauty of green mountains and clear waters, the rural tourism of Hongshan Village has stepped on a fast track in recent years.

广州·黄埔 / 莲塘村

Guangzhou · Huangpu / Liantang Village

莲塘村，背靠玄武山，面向莲花池，池塘似莲藕状，环绕古村，近年来作为“乡村振兴+古村保护”的试点，探索出一条具有黄埔特色的乡村振兴之路。

Liantang Village, with the Xuanwu Mountain at its back and the lotus ponds facing it, is dotted with ponds just like holes on a slice of lotus root. As a pilot of the "rural revitalization + ancient village conservation project" in recent years, the village has explored a rural revitalization path with Huangpu characteristics.

广州·花都 / 港头村

Guangzhou · Huadu / Gangtou Village

广州·番禺 / 大岭村
Guangzhou · Panyu / Daling Village

广州·花都 / 蓝田村

Guangzhou · Huadu / Lantian Village

广州·花都 / 塱头古村

Guangzhou · Huadu / Langtou Ancient Village

新意

New Ideas

新彩广州

RENEWED
CHARM
OF
GUANGZHOU

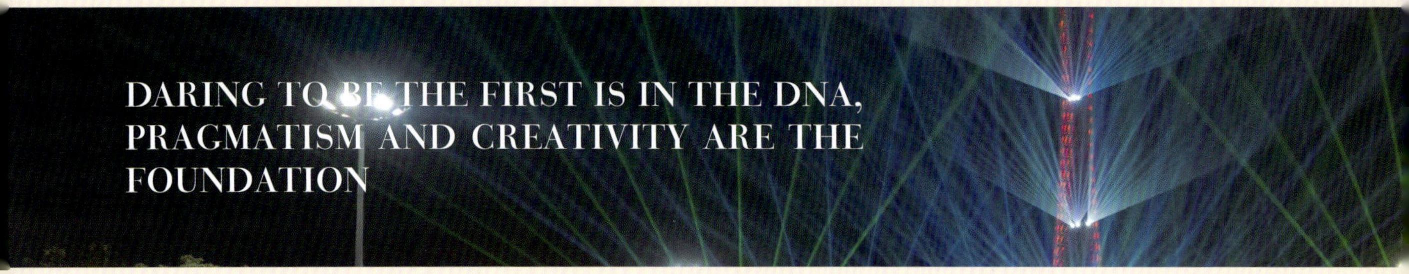

DARING TO BE THE FIRST IS IN THE DNA, PRAGMATISM AND CREATIVITY ARE THE FOUNDATION

Embarking on a new journey, Guangzhou is facing the changes unseen in a hundred years with ambition and confidence.

As a city of creativity, Guangzhou plays the role of a window for foreign exchanges, where Chinese and foreign cultures spread and interact, influencing and integrating with each other.

In recent years, Guangzhou has been accelerating the pace of opening up to the outside world, striving to enhance the city's internationalization and achieving innovations in its cultural sector.

From the International Light Festival, International Documentary Film Festival, Guangzhou Arts Festival, to the Guangzhou Cultural Industry Fair and the Performance Fair, Guangzhou has become an inescapable part of the international performing arts circle, hosting an increasing number of national and international high-end cultural events, and its position as a world-class performance hub is becoming more and more solid.

With its pioneering, pragmatic and innovative spirit, Guangzhou is poised to set sail again.

敢为人先是基因
务实创意是底色

苟日新，日日新，又日新。

踏上新征程，广州正以一种雄姿勃发的姿态面对百年未有之大变局。

作为创意之城，广州从文旅小舞台到城市大舞台，扮演着对外交往的窗口角色，中外文化在这里相互传播与接收，相互影响与融合，川流不息，生生不已。

近年来，广州不断加快对外开放的步伐，着力提升城市国际化水平，在城市文化创意上出新出彩。

从国际灯光节、国际纪录片节、广州艺术节，到文交会、演交会……广州已成为国际演艺版图上不可忽视的重要一站，举办的全国性、国际性高端文化活动日益丰富，广州作为世界级演出集聚地的地位日趋稳固。

敢为人先是其基因，务实创新是其底色。且看，广州擂鼓鸣号，千帆竞发，再起航。

红色之都

Cradle of Revolution

广州是一座英雄城市，近代以来开风气之先，是中国民主革命的策源地。广州是一座有着光荣革命传统、厚重红色文化历史的红色之都。大量的红色遗址掩映在绿树红墙下，见证了这座城市的英雄过往，是广州宝贵的历史文化资源。

Guangzhou is a heroic city which is the birthplace of China's democratic revolution. Guangzhou is a city with glorious revolutionary tradition and profound culture and history. A large number of revolutionary ruins stand under the green trees and red walls, witnessing the city's heroic past and forming precious historical and cultural resources of Guangzhou.

广州·越秀 / 广州起义烈士陵园

Guangzhou · Yuexiu / Guangzhou Uprising Martyrs Cemetery

广州起义烈士陵园为永远缅怀广州起义的丰功伟绩而建，是全国红色旅游经典景区。

Guangzhou Uprising Martyrs Cemetery was built to honor the great achievements of the Guangzhou Uprising. It is a national classic site of red tourism.

广州·黄埔 / 辛亥革命纪念馆

Guangzhou · Huangpu / Memorial Museum of 1911 Revolution

▶

广州·越秀 / 黄花岗烈士陵园

Guangzhou Yuexiu / Huanghuagang Cemetery of the 72 Martyrs

广州·越秀 / 中共三大会址纪念馆

Guangzhou · Yuexiu / The Museum of Site of the 3rd National Congress of the Communist Party of China

广州·越秀 / 农讲所
Guangzhou · Yuexiu / Peasant Movement Institute

广州·黄埔 / 黄埔军校旧址纪念馆

Guangzhou · Huangpu / Whampoa Military Academy Memorial Hall

陸軍
革命尚未
成功

新意

New Ideas

广州·越秀 / 十九路军淞沪抗日阵亡将士陵园

Guangzhou · Yuexiu / Cemetery of Martyrs of the 19th Route Army in the Songhu Anti-Japanese War

广州·越秀 / 广州解放纪念像

Guangzhou · Yuexiu / Guangzhou Liberation Memorial Statue

时尚之都

Fashion Capital

新彩广州，其新意一部分源于时尚。

时尚之都的名号，源于厚实的广州时尚产业。

广州时尚产业集群实力不容小觑。仅白云一区，持证生产化妆品企业数量和占比均位居全国前列，是全国化妆品生产企业数量最多、专业市场发展最早、产业链条最完整的产业集聚区。

现阶段，广州正在打造国际消费中心城市，正是时尚产业集群发挥“千年商都”消费品“产地优势”，抓住国内国际双向循环机遇，实现产业与消费良性互促的好时机。

Some of the new aspects of Guangzhou originate from fashion.

The title of fashion capital comes from the strong fashion industry of the city.

Guangzhou is home of fashion industry clusters. In Baiyun District alone, both the number of licensed cosmetic manufacturing enterprises and their share in the country are among the highest in China. It is an industrial cluster with the largest number of cosmetic manufacturers, the earliest development of professional markets, and the most complete industrial chain in the country.

At present, Guangzhou is building an international consumption city, which is an ideal opportunity for the fashion industry clusters to leverage the advantage of the origin of consumer goods in the thousand-year-old business capital, expand both domestic and international markets, and realize mutual promotion of industry and consumption.

“花开广州　盛放世界”——2023广州文化旅游推介大会

"Blooming in GuangzhouFlourishing around World": 2023 Guangzhou Culture and Tourism Promotion

“读懂中国”国际会议（广州），让世界读懂中国、读懂广东、读懂广州。

The Understanding China Conference（Guangzhou）allows the world to understand Guangzhou, Guangdong and China.

国际灯光节

The International Light Festival

21世纪海上丝绸之路国际博览会，以文旅为媒，促民心相通。

The 21st Century Maritime Silk Road International Expo takes cultural tourism as a medium to promote people-to-people contact.

2023广州国际旅游展览会，吸引了众多市民游客前往。

2023 Guangzhou International Travel Fair attracted many citizens and tourists.

广州 · 天河 / 英迪格酒店

Guangzhou · Tianhe / Hotel Indigo

广州·南沙 / 南沙花园酒店

Guangzhou · Nansha / Nansha Garden Hotel

广州·番禺 / 广东科学中心

Guangzhou · Panyu / Guangdong Science Center

新意 New Ideas

朴实的广州，亦有文艺的一面。

香气四溢的咖啡馆，静谧悠然的老书店，风格奇特的西餐馆，山野深处的新民宿……

底蕴深厚的岭南文化与现代生活的碰撞，丰富了生活的况味，充实着都市人的内心。

Guangzhou, famous for being down-to-earth, also has an artistic side.

In the fragrant cafes, quiet and relaxing old bookstores, stylish western restaurants, new lodges deep in the mountains ...

The deep-rooted Lingnan culture integrates with modern life, enriching the life and minds of urbanites.

文艺之都

Capital of Culture and Art

广州·天河 / 广州大剧院
广东省博物馆
广州图书馆

Guangzhou · Tianhe / Guangzhou Opera House
Guangdong Museum
Guangzhou Library

珠江新城不仅是广州繁华的经济中心，同时也是文化艺术中心。从空中俯瞰，珠江新城的花城广场区域，聚集着广东省博物馆、广州图书馆、广州大剧院等高品质的文化场馆。

Zhujiang New Town is not only the prosperous economic center of Guangzhou, but also the center of culture and art. Looking down from the sky, the Huacheng Plaza area has high-quality cultural venues such as the Guangdong Museum, Guangzhou Library, and Guangzhou Opera House.

广州艺术季，让市民共享艺术文化发展成果。

Guangzhou Art Season allows citizens to share the achievements of art and culture development.

广州插花节

Guangzhou Flower Arranging Festival

广州·南沙 / 南沙图书馆

Guangzhou · Nansha / Nansha Library

广州·海珠 / 小洲村

Guangzhou · Haizhu / Xiaozhou Village

广州文交会，推动区域文化产业对话交流合作，致力于打造粤港澳大湾区综合性文化产业交易平台。

Guangzhou Cultural Industry Fair promotes dialogue, exchange and cooperation in the regional cultural industry and strives to build a comprehensive cultural industry trading platform in the Guangdong-Hong Kong-Macao Greater Bay Area.

中国（广州）国际纪录片节，是中国唯一国家级并享有交易功能的纪录片盛会，最直观地展现了广州的务实和包容。

The China (Guangzhou) International Documentary Film Festival is the only national documentary event in China that provides on-site transaction services, which is most demonstrative of Guangzhou's pragmatism and inclusiveness.

创意之都

Capital of Creativity

新意
New Ideas

作为一个聚集了服装产业设计、纺织、美业、珠宝、科技等众多时尚文化设计产业的城市，广州最不缺的就是创意。依托自身文化底蕴、制造产业基础和经济建设水平，广州以想象力绘就这座国际都市的大未来。

As a city that gathers many fashion, cultural and design industries such as fashion design, textile, beauty industry, jewelry and technology, Guangzhou never lacks in creativity. Leveraging its profound cultural heritage, manufacturing industrial foundation and economic strength, Guangzhou draws the blueprint for this international metropolis with imagination.

广州·白云 / 广州城市规划展览中心
Guangzhou · Baiyun / Guangzhou Urban Planning Exhibition Center

广州·海珠 / 咏声动画科技馆

Guangzhou · Haizhu / Yongsheng Animation Science and Technology Museum

广州·海珠 / 广州地铁博物馆

Guangzhou · Haizhu / Guangzhou Metro Museum

广州国际旅游展览会

Guangzhou International Travel Fair

广州国际旅游展览会，是连续举办30多年的广州旅游品牌节庆活动。作为我国创办历史最早、举办时间最长的大型国际旅游展览会，它为海内外旅游业界搭建交流交易平台，为观众展现最新的旅游发展趋势。

Guangzhou International Travel Fair is a flagship tourism festival held in Guangzhou continuously for over 30 years. As the earliest international travel fair in China, it builds a platform for exchange and trading for the tourism industry at home and abroad, and showcases the latest tourism development trends to visitors.

"羊城之夏"广州市民文化季

Guangzhou Summer City Culture Season

新意

New Ideas

广州·黄埔 / 长洲岛都市农业公园

Changzhou · Huangpu / Changzhou Island Urban Agriculture Park

广州·从化 / 天人山水景区
Guangzhou · Conghua / Tian Ren Shan Shui Tourist Park

自动驾驶出租车“萝卜快跑”在广州投入运营。

Robotaxi Apollo Go has been put into operation in Guangzhou.

小鹏汇天以城市空中出行（UAM）为目标，致力于打造全球最安全的智能电动飞行汽车。
With the goal of urban air mobility (UAM), XPeng Aeroht is committed to building the world's safest intelligent electric flying car.